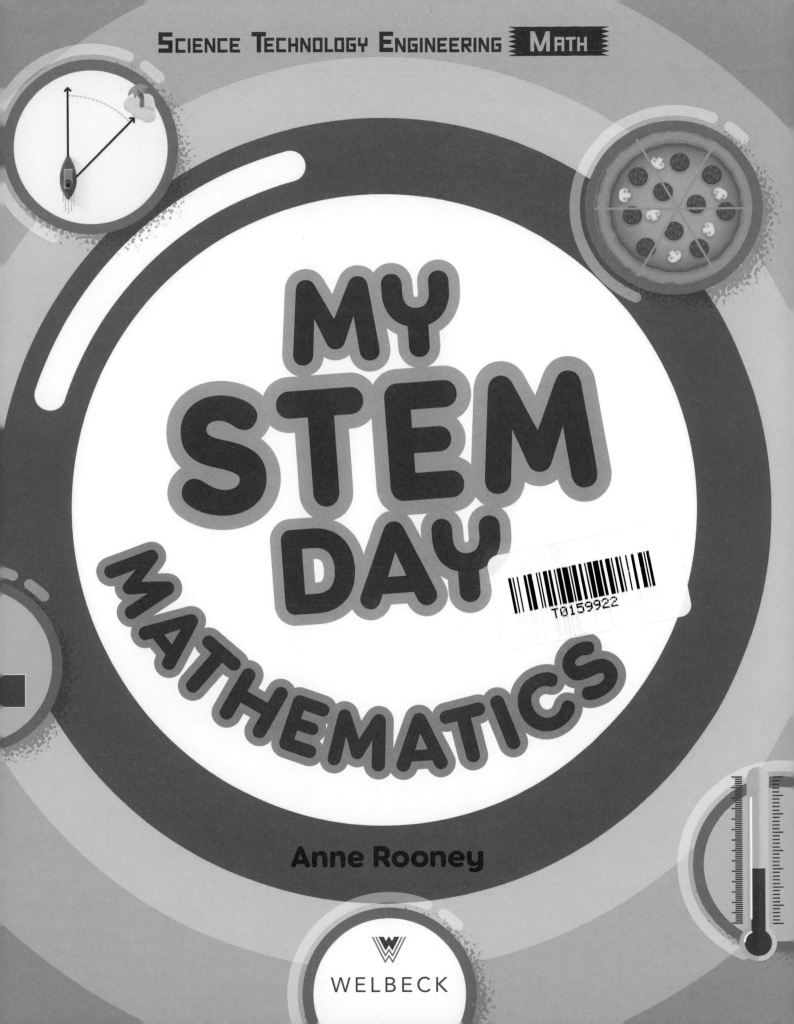

SCIENCE TECHNOLOGY ENGINEERING **MATH**

MY STEM DAY

MATHEMATICS

Anne Rooney

WELBECK

Published in 2021 by Welbeck Children's Books

An Imprint of Welbeck Children's Limited,
part of Welbeck Publishing Group.
20 Mortimer Street London W1T 3JW

Text & Illustrations © Welbeck Children's Limited, part of Welbeck
Publishing Group.

ISBN:978 1 78312 657 6
Printed in Dongguan, China

Design Manager: **Emily Clarke**
Editorial Manager: **Joff Brown**
Executive Editors: **Selina Wood and Nancy Dickmann**
Design: **Jake da'Costa and WildPixel Ltd.**
Picture research: **Steve Behan**
Production: **Nicola Davey**
Editorial Consultant: **Jack Challoner**

FSC
www.fsc.org
MIX
Paper from
responsible sources
FSC® C020056

AUTHOR

Anne Rooney writes about all kinds of science for children and adults.
When not writing books, she can be found getting muddy hunting
for fossils, or travelling around Europe by train looking for dinosaur
museums and the best chocolate ice cream.

STEM CONSULTANT

Jack Challoner has a degree in physics and trained as a science
and maths teacher before moving to the Education Unit at London's
Science Museum. He now writes science and technology books and
performs science shows in museums and schools.

ILLUSTRATOR

Dan@ KJA-artists has been a designer and illustrator for more than 16
years, with his work featured in national magazines and newspapers,
on websites, album covers, adverts, prime time TV and giant billboards.
He's rarely seen without a pen, crayon (he has 3 small children!) or
strong coffee in hand.

Adult supervision is recommended for all activities.

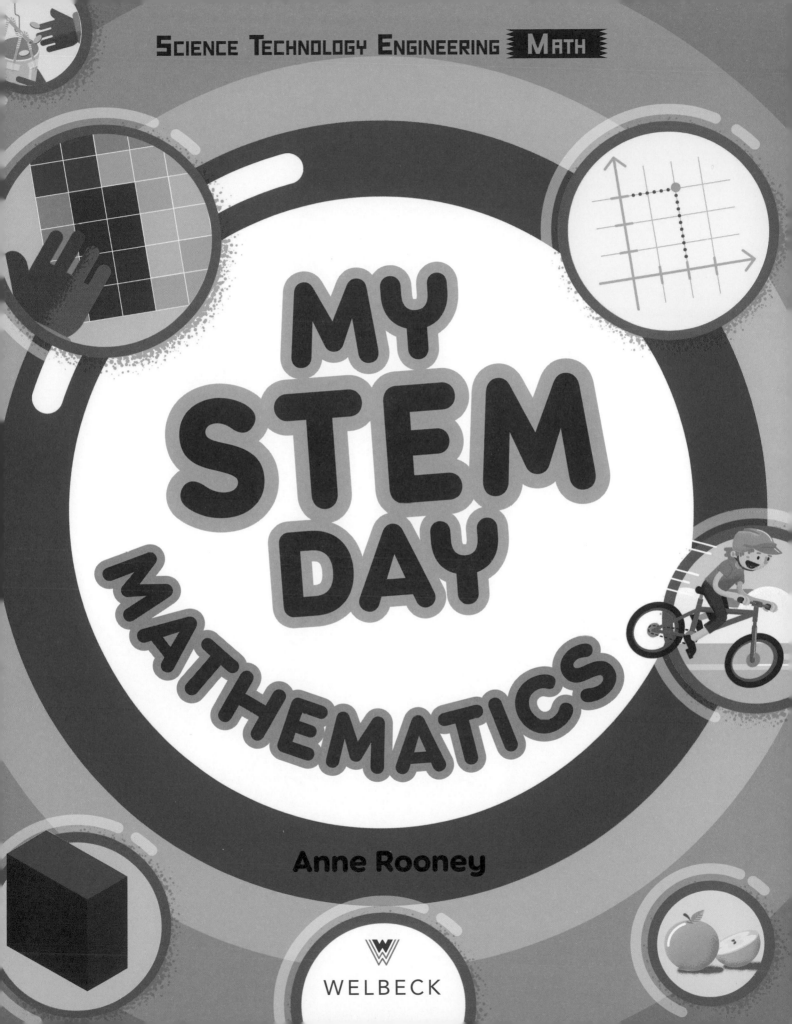

SCIENCE TECHNOLOGY ENGINEERING MATH

MY STEM DAY

MATHEMATICS

Anne Rooney

WELBECK

CONTENTS

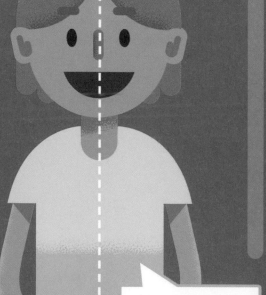

ARE YOU THE SAME ON BOTH SIDES?

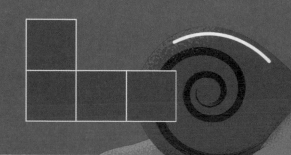

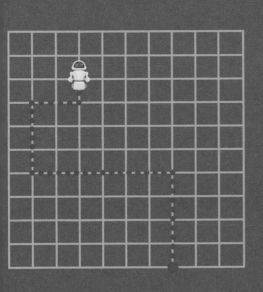

WHAT IS STEM?

STEM is everywhere in our lives. But it's not all about flowers! Instead, STEM is short for **Science**, **Technology**, **Engineering** and **Mathematics**.

Have you ever timed how long a bike journey takes, counted the number of legs on a bug or measured how high you can jump? If so, you've made use of **STEM**. Scientists and mathematicians over the years have used their knowledge and skills to develop tools, structures and processes that we use every day.

Are you curious about the world around you? Do you love to ask questions and try out new ideas? Maybe you're a whiz at spotting patterns, solving problems and finding out how things work. If you try something that doesn't work out the first time, do you try again with a different approach? If so, you'll love the world of **STEM**.

Mathematics, or math for short, is one of the four branches of STEM. It's the study of numbers, measurements and shapes—and a language that people from all over the world can understand. Math can be anything from working out the quantities of ingredients you need to bake a cake, displaying figures on a chart so you can compare them or working out how many bank notes you need to pay for a new toy.

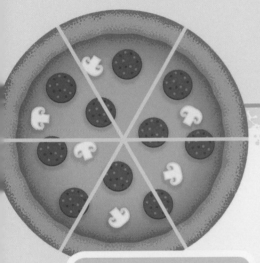

$$1 \div 6 = 1/6$$

We depend on math in our daily lives. We need it to understand train timetables, share out a pizza, know how many tiles will fit in a swimming pool and work out the number of stars in the sky! Once you know where to look, you'll spot math everywhere you go!

What about the rest of **STEM**? Well, **Science** investigates the natural world. **Technology** is about making useful devices and new processes. **Engineering** is all about solving problems to create structures and machines. These subjects work together to explore and create incredible things!

THE STEM DAY TEAM

SCIENCE   TECHNOLOGY   ENGINEERING   MATH

Time to wake up!

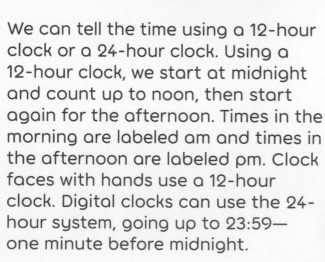

What time do you get up?

You might be told it's too late on a school day—or too early on the weekend if everyone else wants to sleep in!

We split the day into 24 hours, and each hour into 60 minutes. We split each minute into 60 seconds. The Ancient Babylonians first came up with this method—they used 6 and 60 a lot in their number system and it has stuck.

We can tell the time using a 12-hour clock or a 24-hour clock. Using a 12-hour clock, we start at midnight and count up to noon, then start again for the afternoon. Times in the morning are labeled am and times in the afternoon are labeled pm. Clock faces with hands use a 12-hour clock. Digital clocks can use the 24-hour system, going up to 23:59—one minute before midnight.

You can figure out how long you slept by subtracting your bedtime from midnight and adding the hours you have slept since midnight. So if you went to bed at 8 pm, that's 4 hours before midnight. And if you got up at 7:30 am, that's 7.5 hours after midnight.

We can use time to measure speed. You can work out speed by dividing the distance something travels by the time it takes to get there. So if you walk **300 steps in 3 minutes**, your speed is **100 paces per minute**. We often report speeds in miles per hour (mph) or kilometers per hour (km/h).

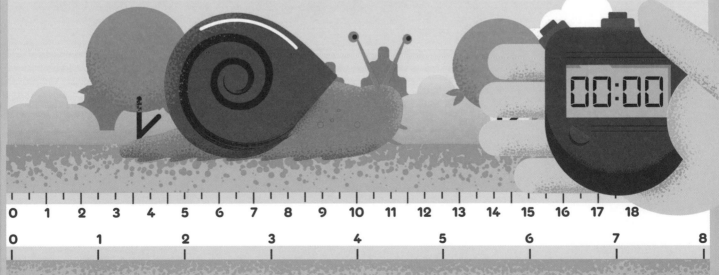

How do you spend your day?

BEEP! BEEP!

How well do you keep track of time? Does it always seem like you don't have enough time to do everything you want to do? Or do you sit around being bored half the day? Find out what you really do with your time.

What to do:

1. Time all the activities that you do regularly. How long is the journey to school? How long to brush your teeth? How much time do you spend using the bathroom? If it's a school day, how long are your classes? What about eating? And how long do you sleep? What about using the computer, or watching TV, or reading? Write down all the times.

2. When you have the times for a whole day, use your graph paper to make a graph.

3. Draw a rectangle on the graph paper 24 x 30 squares. Each square represents two minutes of your day. Each row of 30 squares is an hour.

4. Starting with the thing you spent most time doing (probably sleeping!), color in squares for all your activities. If you slept for ten hours, that's **60 x 10 = 600 minutes**, so color in 300 squares: ten rows of 30 squares.

5. Use a different color for each activity.

6. How many white squares are left at the end? Multiply by 2 to find out how many minutes you haven't counted. What could you do with that time?

Now think of your perfect day. What would you do and where would you go? Write down the times for each activity and draw another graph to show them.

HMM!

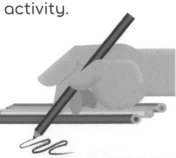

Puzzle activity

Olivia leaves the house at 4 pm. Fill in the clocks to show what time she finishes each activity. The first one is done for you.

Wait for bus: 10 mins	On the bus: 25 mins	In the cinema: 1 hour 50 minutes	Walk to restaurant: 5 mins	Eat pizza: 50 mins

①

②

③

④

⑤

Clock 1: `04:10`

Clocks 2–5: `88:88`

Looking good!

Check the mirror to make sure there's no toothpaste on your chin before school. Have you noticed how your reflection looks the same as you—but the other way round? It's an example of a transformation.

Transformation changes an object without altering its size or shape—so all lines are the same length and all angles the same size before and after the change.

A reflection is the same image, but flipped to be the other way around. An image and its reflection are symmetrical—made of identical parts that face each other. Something can be reflected horizontally or vertically. You see a vertical reflection if you look at a bird swimming on water.

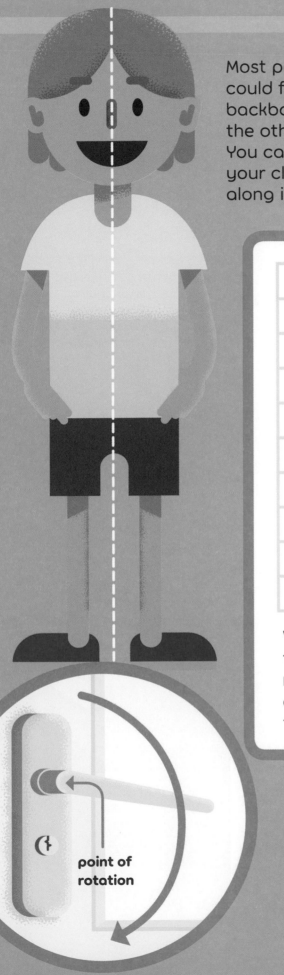

Most people are symmetrical. If you could fold yourself in half along your backbone, one half would exactly cover the other with no gaps or overlaps. You can see this when you fold your clothes. The line you fold them along is called the axis of symmetry.

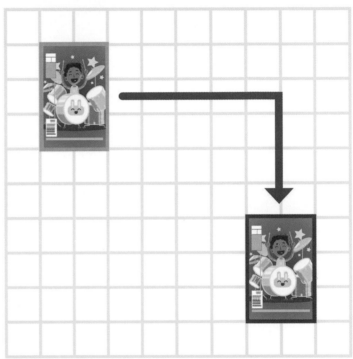

When a shape is translated it is moved to a new position without resizing, rotating, or flipping. If you slide a comic or glass along a table, that's a translation.

point of rotation

When a shape rotates, one point stays in the same place and the rest turns around that point. If you turn it all the way round, through 360 degrees, it goes back to how it was at the start.

You will need:

- graph paper (¼ in/0.5 cm squares are ideal)
- scissors
- colored pens or pencils

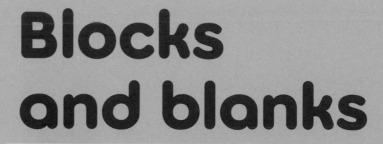

You can make a game that uses translations to fit blocks together. It's called Tetris. You might have played it on a computer or phone.

What to do:

1. Copy the shapes below onto the squared paper. You will need five or more copies of each shape.

2. Color them (on both sides) to make your game look more interesting and so that you can tell the shapes apart quickly. Then cut them out.

3. Now try to put them together to make a solid block with no gaps, or as few gaps as possible. You can translate, rotate, and reflect the shapes to get them to fit together.

4. Work as quickly as you can! You could time yourself and see how quickly you can do it.

Puzzle activity

Take a look at these animal pictures. Can you tell which animals have been rotated and which have been reflected?

1

2
3
4

Don't get lost!

You probably know the way to school. But if someone new moved next door, you might have to give them directions, describing a route using distances and angles.

TURN 45 DEGREES EAST, THEN SAIL 50 KM!

If you were in a boat at sea, you could travel in a straight line to where you wanted to go. To give instructions, you would give the angle (how much you need to turn), and how far to go. But on the way to school, you have to follow the roads, going one way and then another.

45°

island

boat

North 0°

West 90°

East 90°

South 180°

We describe a route by giving directions and distances. The distances can be in any units: paces, feet, yards, miles.

Directions can be left, right, forward, backward, the points of the compass (north, east, south, west), or in degrees.

Sometimes pairs of numbers are used to specify a single point. These numbers are called coordinates and in math they can be plotted on a grid with "x" and "y" lines. Here, the coordinates 2,3 mean the point is 2 squares along the horizontal line (called the x-axis) and 3 squares up the vertical line (the y-axis). Only one point matches the coordinates.

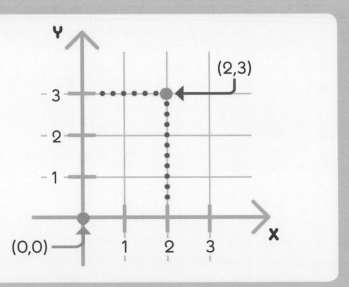

Clear instructions are the basis of computer programming, too. You might learn simple programming using a small robot that you can direct with instructions like:

Up 4, Left 6, Up 3, Right 2, Up 1.

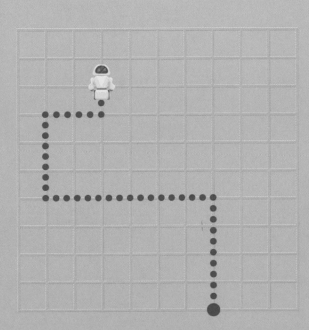

Sets of instructions are called algorithms and they are at the heart of all computer programs. A computer needs clear, detailed instructions that cover every single step of a process. It can't make a guess if something is missing or not precise.

Up 4, Left 6, Up £, Right 2, Up 1.

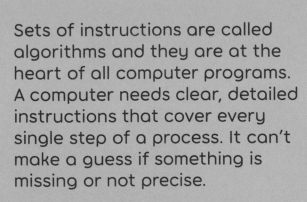

ERROR!

You will need:

- a friend
- an open space
- ingredients for a snack, such as bread, butter, ham, cheese, or anything you like!

How good are you at writing instructions? Driverless cars follow instructions to get from one place to another—could you program your friend to work like a driverless car? Or to work as a robot?

What to do:

1. While your friend is not looking, pace out a route from a starting point to a destination—it could be from the monkey bars to the swings in a playground. Write down your route as instructions like this: "Forward 5 steps; turn left; walk 6 steps; turn right; walk 4 steps..."

2. Stand your friend at the starting position and shout out the instructions, one at a time. Did they work? Did the friend get to the right place?

TURN RIGHT!

3. Wouldn't it be great to have a robot that could make you a snack? Think through all the stages of making a sandwich. Your robot won't do anything that you don't tell it to do, even things like picking up the knife or taking the lid off a jar!

HMM!

4. Write really precise and clear instructions. Collect all the stuff that will be needed and then give your friend the instructions to follow. Tell them not to make any guesses and not to do anything that's not in the instructions. Do you get a sandwich?

Puzzle activity

Which treat will the mouse get if it follows these instructions?

Finish

Start

> up 1; right 1; up 2; left 1; up 2; left 1; down 1; left 1; up 1; left 3

Write your own instructions to help the mouse get home to the mouse hole after its snack.

Write your answer here

....

....

....

....

Out and about

Do you have to go up or down a hill on your way to school or to the store? Or is your route flat? The world is full of lumps and bumps. And there's water, too, which evens out over the whole world.

When we measure the altitude (height) of land, the level of the sea is counted as zero. Most land is above sea level, but everything under the sea is below sea level.

Numbers go below zero as well as above. Numbers below zero are negative numbers and have a minus sign (-) in front of them. To measure distances below sea level (below zero), we use negative numbers.

Using a number line makes it easy to do calculations with negative numbers. Negative numbers are to the left of zero and positive numbers are to the right.

-10 -9 -8 -7 -6 -5 -4 -3 -2 -1 0 1 2 3 4 5 6 7 8 9 10

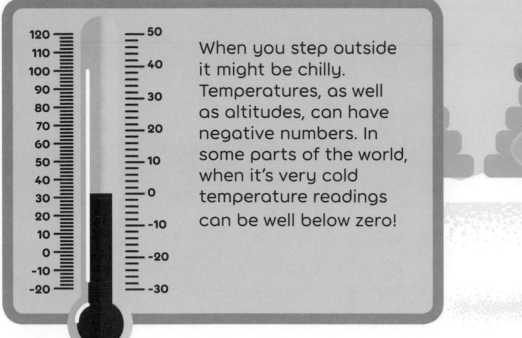

When you step outside it might be chilly. Temperatures, as well as altitudes, can have negative numbers. In some parts of the world, when it's very cold temperature readings can be well below zero!

 plus sheep

 minus sheep

Negative numbers are also used for counting. Imagine a farmer has 10 sheep. She puts a pebble into a pot as each of her sheep comes home. By nightfall, 7 sheep are home and 3 are missing. She has 7 pebbles in the "plus sheep" pot and 3 spare pebbles. She can think of them as "minus sheep".

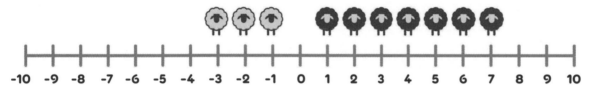

If another sheep wanders off, that's **7 — 1 = 6** "plus sheep". But the extra missing sheep increases the number of "minus sheep" to -4.

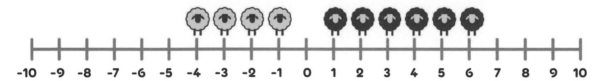

If 2 missing sheep come back, we are taking away 2 from the -4 sheep, leaving -2 sheep still missing: **-4 — -2 = -2.** When subtracting a negative number, the two "minuses" cancel out and you add the number instead. You're taking away some of the things that have been taken away!

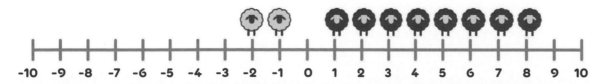

Out to sea!

Take a look at this underwater scene. Each creature is at a different altitude or depth. Use these figures to work out the answers to the questions.

seal -3 ft

How far must each creature move up (+) or down (-) for:

1. the shark to eat the common octopus?

....

2. the seal to eat the box jellyfish?

....

3. the bird to catch the angelfish?

....

4. the sperm whale to eat the octopus?

....

5. the manta ray to get to the surface?

....

6. the shark to attack the bird?

....

box jellyfish -20 ft

manta ray -40 ft

sperm whale -90 ft

bird 10 ft

angelfish -10 ft

sea turtle -30 ft

common octopus -60 ft

great white shark -80 ft

You'll find the answers at the back of the book.

10 ft

0

-10 ft

-20 ft

-30 ft

-40 ft

-50 ft

-60 ft

-70 ft

-80 ft

-90 ft

-100 ft

Running around

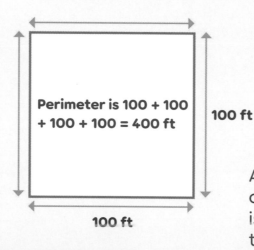

It's time for sport and you might be going for a run. How can you tell how far you have run if you go all around the school playing field?

HUFF!
PUFF!

The distance around the edge of a shape is called its perimeter. To work it out, you add up the lengths of all the sides. It's easy to work out the perimeter of a square as all four sides are the same length.

Perimeter is 100 + 100 + 100 + 100 = 400 ft

100 ft

100 ft

Perimeter is 50 + 100 + 50 + 100 = 200 ft

50 ft

100 ft

A rectangle has two pairs of equal sides. The perimeter is twice the width plus twice the length.

You can work out the perimeter of an odd shape by adding together all the sides.

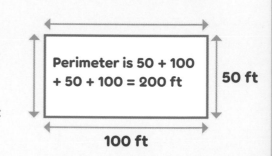

15 ft
6 ft
9 ft
9 ft
9 ft
9 ft
3 ft
9 ft
6 ft
3 ft
3 ft
9ft
3 ft
9 ft

Perimeter is:

15   9   9   3   3   9   9   9   3   3   3   6   9   9 + 6 = 96 ft

The space inside a shape is the area. To work out the area of a square or rectangular shape, multiply the length by the width, using the same units of measurement (such as inches, feet, centimeters, or meters). Area is given in "square" units, such as inches or square centimeters. Square inches are written as in^2. A square inch is the area inside a square with sides of one inch.

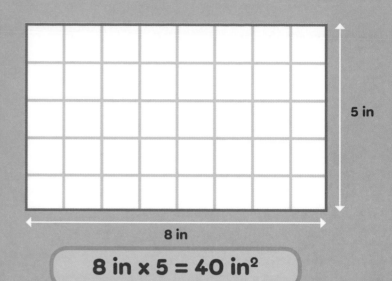

5 in

8 in

$$8 \text{ in} \times 5 = 40 \text{ in}^2$$

A: square field, 10 x 10, perimeter 40, area 100

B: rectanglular field, 4 x 25, perimeter 58, area 100

C: rectangular field, 18 x 2, perimeter 40, area 36

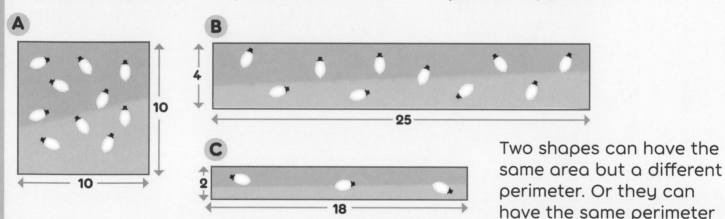

A

10

10

B

4

25

C

2

18

Two shapes can have the same area but a different perimeter. Or they can have the same perimeter but a different area.

You can work out the perimeter of a more complicated shape by putting string around it and then measuring the string.

You will need:

- graph paper
- plastic construction blocks
- colored pens

When someone builds a house, they want to get as much useful space inside as they can for the smallest perimeter—the building materials for the walls cost money! But they also have to fit it into the area they have available, and they might want it to be an interesting shape. You can experiment with different shaped buildings, too!

What to do:

1. Using the construction blocks, lay out the plan of a room on the graph paper. Draw around the outline on the graph paper using a colored pen. Count the squares on the paper to calculate the perimeter (some blocks may end on a half or quarter of a square). Figure out the area. Write the area and perimeter beside the outline, using the same color pen.

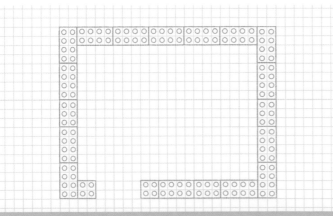

2. Rearrange the same number of construction blocks to make a different room. Draw around it again, using a different color, and work out the perimeter and area.

3. Keep trying different shapes. If you can't easily work out the area of a shape you make, you can count the squares to find the area.

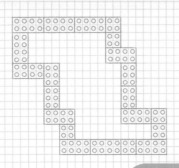

4. Which shape gives the largest area?

The simplest shapes give more area for least perimeter. The best of all is a circle!

 # Puzzle activity

This sports track has different routes for younger children and older children. If each square represents 1 foot, find out how far children of each age have to run by working out the perimeter of the different ro utes. Then color another route around the track and work out how far it is.

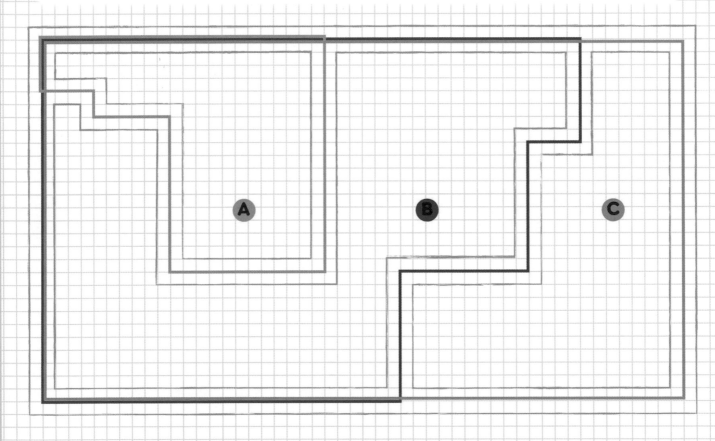

A

B

C

Fair shares

We often have to share things—especially at meal times. To share food at lunchtime, you might have to divide larger things into smaller equal pieces.

When you share things evenly, you have to work with fractions and division. A fraction is a part of a whole. A half is a fraction: when we divide one thing into two equal parts, each part is a half.

To write a fraction, we put the number of whole objects above a line and the number we are dividing it by—the number of shares there are—underneath. The top number is called the numerator. The bottom number is called the denominator:

$$\frac{\text{Numerator}}{\text{Denominator}}$$

If you have one pizza and six people, it's clear you need to cut it into six pieces and have one sixth each. This is a simple fraction: $1 \div 6 = \frac{1}{6}$.

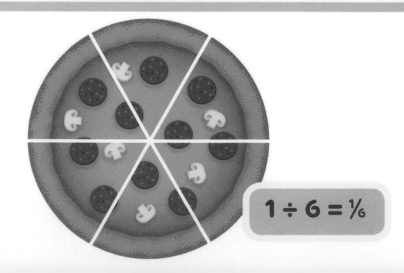

$$1 \div 6 = \frac{1}{6}$$

But what if you have two pizzas and six people? The numerator is 2, and the denominator is 6, so ²⁄₆ . You can divide both the top and bottom of this fraction by 2, making ⅓ . That is called simplifying the fraction.

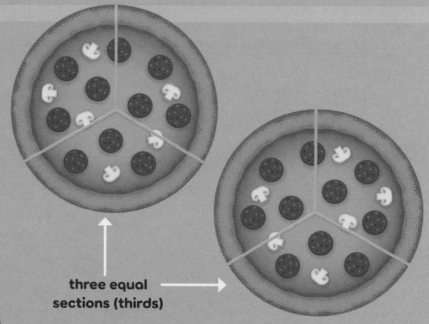

three equal sections (thirds)

If you have more food than people, you might be able to divide the food exactly. After you've eaten the pizza, you and your five friends could easily share 18 strawberries:

you'd have three each as
18 ÷ 6 = 3

3 strawberries each

Sometimes, you might get a mix of whole things and fractions. If you and five friends share 9 apples:

that's
⁹⁄₆ = ³⁄₂ – or 1 ½
apples each.

You will need:

- a friend
- a pencil and lots of paper
- 6 small index cards

Play this game to have fun with a friend while practising with fractions.

What to do:

1. First, make some cards with fractions written on them. Write each of these fractions on one of the cards: ½ ⅓ ¼ ⅕ ⅔ ¾

½ ⅓ ¼

⅕ ⅔ ¾

2. Mix up the cards and put them in a pile, face down.

face down

3. Choose which of you will draw first and which will guess. If you're drawing, take the top card without showing your companion. It'll tell you the fraction to draw.

4. Think of an object that you can draw a fraction of, and start sketching it on the paper, where your friend can see it. You might draw half a shark, or a third of tree. Don't say what you are drawing. Your companion has to guess the object and the fraction you are drawing as quickly as they can, while you're still drawing.

half a shark

two thirds of a tree

5. Once your friend has tried to guess your drawing they should finish the drawing off. For instance, if you've drawn a quarter of a cake, they need to draw another three quarters. Did they finish the drawing correctly?

6. Swap roles, so next time your friend picks a card off the pile and draws first.

Puzzle activity

You want to use a quarter of the beads to make a necklace. In each jar, color in a quarter of the beads. Use a different color for each jar.

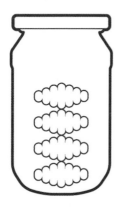 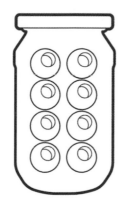 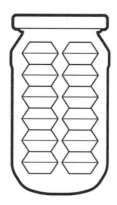  

In this space, draw the necklace you would make with your beads. Now color in a third of the remaining beads in a different color. What fraction of the beads are uncolored?

You're 100%!

Your grade for a school test might be shown as a fraction or a percentage. If you get 10 out of 10, you've got it all correct, and you have 100 per cent!

Percentages split a whole group or object into 100 parts. Each part is $\frac{1}{100}$, or 1 per cent (%). To convert a fraction to a percentage, multiply the numerator by 100 and then divide by the denominator.

So ½ as a percentage is:

$100 \div 2 = 50\%$, ¼ is $100 \div 4 = 25\%$ and ¾ is $300 \div 4 = 75\%$

Percentages are a more flexible way of showing parts than fractions. A fraction like $\frac{37}{50}$ is hard to think about. But if we write it as $\frac{75}{100}$, or 74%, it's clear that it's about three quarters.

TEST RESULTS

90%

Scientists often report their results as percentages. It's an easy way of showing proportions even when they are not exact fractions.

Fish populations

70%

30%

It's easy to do sums with different fractions if you convert them to percentages. A sum like ¾ + ⅕ looks really hard. But convert both to percentages and it becomes easy:

75% + 20% = 95%

YES!

Sometimes you'll see special offers like "20% off". To work out how much you can save, multiply the full price by the discount and divide by 100. If a pair of trainers is $40, with 20% off, the sum is:

20% OFF

$40 x 20 ÷ 100 = 800 ÷ 100 = $8 off
You would have to pay **$40 − $8 = $32**

Sometimes information you get from fractions or percentages can be displayed on charts. Pie charts show how a whole group can be divided into "slices" of pie. The size of each slice depends on what proportion (such as fraction or percentage) it is of the whole group. This pie chart shows favorite flavors of fruit juice in a class of children.

Favourite fruit juices of a class

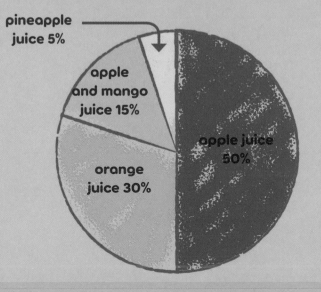

pineapple juice 5%

apple and mango juice 15%

apple juice 50%

orange juice 30%

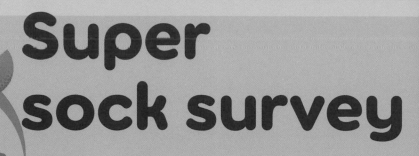

Super sock survey

Practise working out fractions and turning them into percentages by carrying out a survey—of your very own sock drawer!

What to do:

1. What color is each of your socks? Pick the main color for each sock and draw up a chart showing the number of each color.

main color: red

main color: blue

Color of sock	Fraction	Number of socks	Percentage
Blue		5	
Red		6	
Black		3	
Yellow		2	

2. Draw around a plate to make a circle on a piece of paper. Draw straight lines across the middle of the circle to divide it into halves and then quarters. Draw another two lines to cut the quarters in half, making eighths. Then divide the eighths in half making sixteenths.

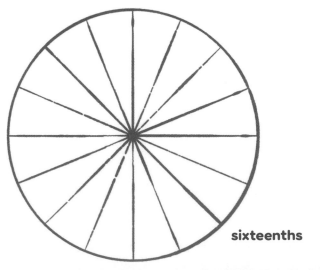

sixteenths

4 blue socks = 4 segments

3. Color in the right number of segments (next to each other) for each set of socks. For example, if you have four blue socks, color four parts of the circle blue.

4. Work out the fraction for each color and write it on your chart. To find the percentage, take the number of segments and multiply by 6.25.

Puzzle activity

These people are visiting the vet with their pets. Look carefully at the picture and count how many animals there are in total. How many of each type? Work out what percentage of each type of animal there is.

Total number of animals is ....

Dogs..............%   Birds.......................%

Cats..............%   Guinea pigs ....%

Snakes.........%   Tortoises..............%

You'll find the answers at the back of the book.

What are the chances?

In drama lesson, everyone is going to dress as a superhero. What are the chances you'll get to wear your favourite color cape? You can work it out using probability.

TA-DAH!

Probability measures the chance of something happening. If an event is certain, the probability is 1: the probability there will be a Saturday this week is 1. If there is no chance of something happening, the probability is 0: the probability there will be two Tuesdays this week is 0.

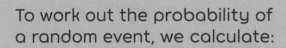
Saturday

To work out the probability of a random event, we calculate:

Number of ways the event can happen
———————————————————————
Number of possible events

If you toss a coin, the probability of it coming down heads is 1/2 because there is one way of getting heads and two possible outcomes: heads or tails. If there are **30** superhero capes and **5** are red, the probability of getting a red one if you go first and they are picked randomly is 5/30, which is 5/6.

If you throw a die, the probability of getting a **5** is 1/6. If you throw the die again, the chance is 1/6 again—the result the second time is unaffected by the result the first time. But if you want to work out the chances of both A and B happening together you multiply the individual probabilities. So the chances of you throwing a **5** and then your friend throwing a **5** is $1/6 \times 1/6 = 1/36$.

Now, if you are the second person to get a superhero cape, the probability of getting a red one has changed from 5/30 because one cape has gone. If the first person took a red one, there are only **4** red capes out of **29**, so the probability is 4/29. If the first person took a blue one, the probability is 5/29 as there are still **5** red capes left.

Testing probability

You will need:

- a friend to play with (or do it alone)
- an even set of small objects in two colors, such as counters, marbles, or candy. Ideally 40 objects but you can use fewer
- 2 bowls to put them in
- a pencil and paper

Now you can explore probability for yourself with a few household objects and a friend!

What to do:

1. Divide the colored objects between the two bowls, with equal numbers of each color in each bowl.

2. Close your eyes and take an object out of one bowl, and have your friend will take one out of the other bowl. Before you do that, draw a chart like this:

You	Your friend	Ticks
Red	Red	
Red	Blue	
Blue	Red	
Blue	Blue	

3. Now think, what is the probability that you will take a red object? What is the probability your friend will take red? Can you work out the probability that you will both take red? What is the probability that at least one of you will take a red object? What is the probability that only one of you will take red?

4. Return the objects to the bowl. Then both of you should close your eyes, take one object each and put a check mark next to the combination of colors you get on the chart.

5. This time, you must take an object before your friend. Starting from here, what's the probability that your friend will take the same color? When one of the objects has been chosen, the probability changes. Put a check next to the combination you get this time.

6. Keep taking and returning objects, and checking the boxes until you have had 20 turns each. Add up the checks for each color combination row. How closely do your scores match predictions for:

- **both of you getting red**
- **at least one of you getting red**
- **only one of you getting red?**

Puzzle activity

Using four different colors, color in the beetles so that there is a probability of ⅟₇ of the child with the bug viewer picking up a green one. What are the probabilities of getting each of the other colors you have used? Draw and color more beetles to make the probability of getting a green one ⅛.

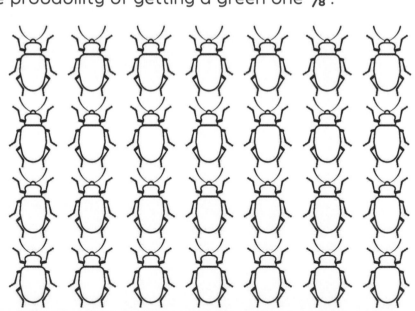

Swinging by the store

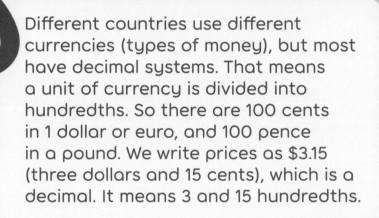

If you buy a snack or a comic on the way home from school you use money to pay for it. Let's take a closer look at how money works.

Different countries use different currencies (types of money), but most have decimal systems. That means a unit of currency is divided into hundredths. So there are 100 cents in 1 dollar or euro, and 100 pence in a pound. We write prices as $3.15 (three dollars and 15 cents), which is a decimal. It means 3 and 15 hundredths.

Amounts less than a dollar, pound, or euro can be written either as a decimal —such as **$0.35** or **£0.10**—or as whole numbers of pence or cents: **35¢** or **10p**.

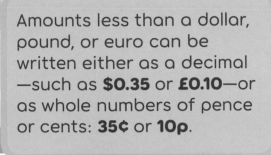

£0.35   35p

When paying for something, you have to choose the right coins to have the amount you need. It's just simple addition, but you can only use the coins available. The coins in US currency are **$1, 50¢, 25¢, 10¢, 5¢**, and **1¢**. British coins are **£2, £1, 50p, 20p, 10p, 5p, 2p**, and **1p**. Euros are **€2, €1, 50c, 20c, 10c, 5c, 2c**, and **1c**. There are bills for larger amounts, like **5, 10, 20**, and **50**.

If you don't have the right money, you have to give more than the price and get change. To work out the change you should get, subtract the price from the amount you paid:

2.45

£5

5.00 − 2.45 = 2.55
bill − price = change
Each time the number goes over 100, we increase the number of dollars, pounds, or euros: so **75¢ + 40¢ = 115¢ = $1.15**

Make a fortune!

You will need:

- an adult to help
- cardboard
- a mug to draw around
- scissors
- a toothpick
- a ruler
- colored pens or pencils
- a pencil and paper to keep score

Here's a game to play with a friend using a coin spinner. Who can make a pile of money first?

Sharp scissors! WATCH OUT!

What to do:

1. Draw around the mug to make a circle on the cardboard. Cut it out carefully.

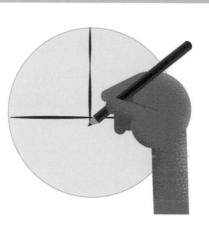

2. Using the ruler and a pen, find the widest width across the circle and draw lines across to divide the circle into four equal parts.

3. Draw sums of money in each quarter, made up from a mix of different coins.

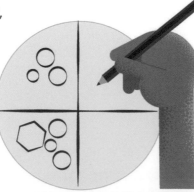

4. Ask an adult to help you push the toothpick through the center of the spinner. Make sure it's exactly in the center, or your spinner might not spin well.

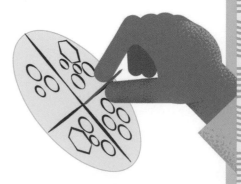

5. Choose how much you want to set as the winning amount—maybe $3 or $5.

6. Spin the spinner. Add up the money shown in the part that rests on the ground and write it on your score chart.

7. Take turns spinning, keeping track of how much money you earn on each spin. The winner is the first to get to your target sum.

Puzzle activity

You have **$5** to spend on presents to put in friends' party bags. Can you afford all of these things? What could you buy that would come to exactly **$5**?

Beside each item you pick, list the coins you could use to make that amount.

pencil	$0.15	....
toy monster	$2.25	....
ball	$0.65	....
bubbles	$0.55	....
key ring	$1.05	....
zoo animals	$2.95	....
sweet	$0.10	....
party blower	$0.25	....
balloon	$0.05	....

Total   = ...

You'll find the answers at the back of the book.

Make a model

At home or school, when you draw a picture or make a model, you don't make it as big as the real thing. You make it look the same, but smaller.

We do this using scale. Each measurement in the drawing or model represents a measurement in real life, but scaled up or down. If you draw something half its actual length and width, you are using a scale of **1:2** (say this as "one to two"). That means every **1 in** in the drawing represents **2 in** in the original.

1:2

HALF THE SIZE IS 1:2!

Maps and plans are drawn to scale. You can measure something on the drawing and work out what the corresponding size will be in real life. The same scale is used for all measurements.

You can use scale the other way around, making a drawing or model bigger than the original. If you drew a beetle, you could use a scale of **4:1** to draw it four times as large as the real beetle.

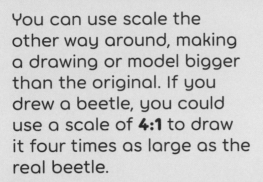

Scale is shown as a ratio. Ratios give us a way of comparing quantities. We often use ratios when cooking. If a cookie recipe calls for equal amounts of butter and sugar, and **1.5 times** as much flour, we can write this as a triple ratio: **1:1:1.5** or, in whole numbers, as **2:2:3** for sugar:butter:flour. The proportions will work, whether you use ounces, cups, or even wheelbarrows full of ingredients!

How tall is a tree?

You will need:

- a friend to help
- a tape measure
- a calculator
- a tree in an area of clear ground
- a sunny day

HMM!

You can use ratios
to work out the size of things that are hard to measure. How else would you measure the height of a tree?

What to do:

1. Stand outside on a sunny day. Find a spot where your shadow falls on clear ground. Ask a friend to measure the length of your shadow.

2. If you don't know how tall you are, ask your friend to measure you, too.

3. Using a calculator, divide your height by the length of your shadow. For example, if you are **60 in** tall and your shadow is **30 in** long, the result is **2**. The ratio of you to your shadow is **2:1**.

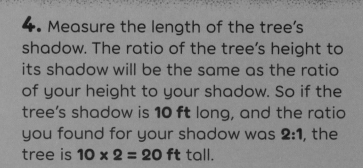

4. Measure the length of the tree's shadow. The ratio of the tree's height to its shadow will be the same as the ratio of your height to your shadow. So if the tree's shadow is **10 ft** long, and the ratio you found for your shadow was **2:1**, the tree is **10 x 2 = 20 ft** tall.

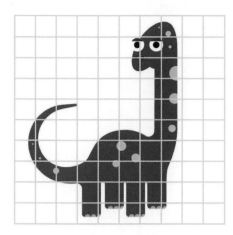

Puzzle activity

Using the grid, copy the drawing on the left at three times the size. You will need to copy the bit in each square exactly into the corresponding larger square. The large squares have sides three times as long as the sides of the small squares.

MAKE IT A DIFFERENT COLOR!

Going for a dip

Have you noticed that when you get in the bath, the water level goes up? That's because you occupy space—you have volume.

SPLOSH!

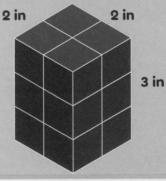

Volume is a measure of the space something takes up, or the amount a container can hold. We measure volume in cubic units, such as cubic inches or cubic centimeters, or in units like gallons, pints, or liters. A gallon is equal to 231 cubic inches.

To work out the volume of a cube or cuboid, multiply **height x width x length**. For a cube, these are all the same, so it's **side x side x side**. A cubic inch (often written in^3) is the volume taken up by a cube with sides of 1 inch.

1 in

$$1 \text{ in} \times 1 \text{ in} \times 1 \text{ in} = 1 \text{ in}^3$$

2 in   2 in

3 in

$$2 \text{ in} \times 3 \text{ in} \times 2 \text{ in} = 12 \text{ in}^3$$

It's harder to work out the volume of other shapes, especially completely irregular shapes. But just as you push water out of the way when you get in the bath, you can measure the water pushed out of the way by an object to find out its volume.

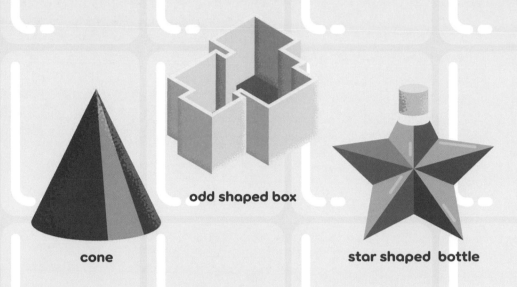

cone

odd shaped box

star shaped bottle

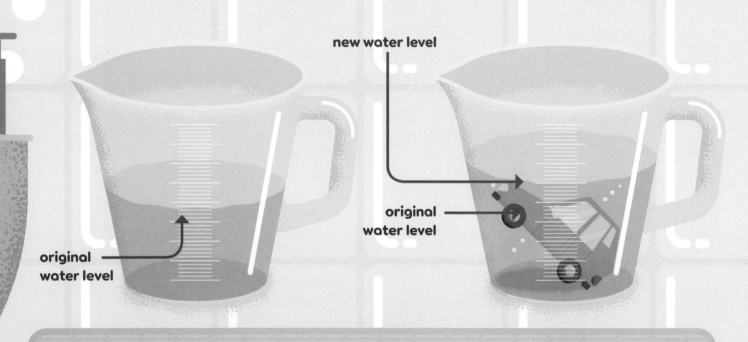

new water level

original water level

original water level

An object has the same volume even if you change its shape. A pile of sugar cubes has the same volume if you rearrange them. A pint of milk still occupies a pint if you spill it— it just has a large area and very little depth.

How big is your hand?

You will need:

- a measuring cup
- water
- small objects that will fit in the cup and won't be ruined if you get them wet, such as an apple, a small plastic toy, a pencil and a sock
- a skewer
- a pencil, ruler and paper

You can measure the volume of lots of objects with irregular shapes by submerging them in water.

What to do:

1. Copy the chart below, filling in the names of the objects you are going to measure.

Object	Hand		
Starting volume	8 oz		
Final volume	12 oz		
Object volume	4 oz		

2. Add water to the measuring cup until it is about half full. Make sure the water level comes to one of the lines marked on the side so that you can read off the volume exactly. Write the starting volume in the second row of your chart.

3. Put your hand into the measuring cup. Where does the water level come to now? Write this volume in the third row of the table.

4. Subtract the figure in row 3 (volume with object submerged) from the figure in row 2 (starting volume) and write the answer in row 4.

5. Remove your hand, top up the water to the original level if you need to, and put the first of your collected objects into the water. If the object floats, push it under water with the skewer and read off the water level when it is submerged. Fill in columns 2, 3 and 4.

6. Repeat for all your objects. If the water overflows, start again for that object with less water in the jug.

Messy! WATCH OUT!

Puzzle activity

Which of these boxes would be the best size to hold **125 cubic inches** of glitter? Decorate it with wrapping paper and a bow.

A

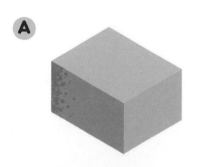

5 in x 4 in x 3 in

B

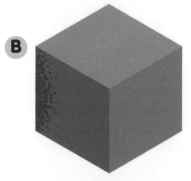

5 in x 5 in x 5 in

C

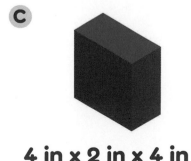

4 in x 2 in x 4 in

D

4 in x 3 in x 2 in

You'll find the answers at the back of the book.

Tile-tastic

Look at the bathroom wall and floor when you get ready for bed. Are they tiled? Tiles can fit together exactly in a pattern that leaves no gaps.

In math, a repeated pattern with no gaps is called a tessellation. Squares and rectangles fit together easily and most tiles are this shape. A brick wall is made of tessellating rectangles.

Triangles and hexagons fit with no gaps, too. Bees make honeycomb from hexagons. It makes a strong structure with no wasted space.

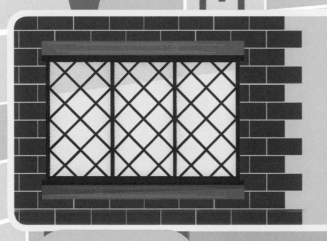

There are lots of examples of tessellated shapes in nature, such as the scales on a snake or a crocodile's teeth.

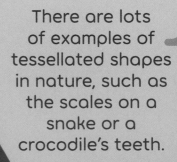

Some tessellations use more than one shape fitted together. They may use irregular shapes, even some with curved lines. Shapes can be transformed (rotated, reflected or moved) to fit together perfectly. They can fit side by side, or be rotated around a central point.

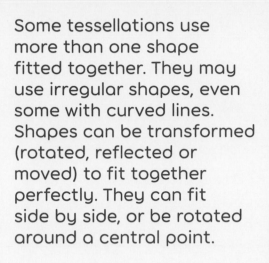

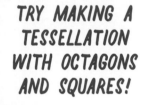

TRY MAKING A TESSELLATION WITH OCTAGONS AND SQUARES!

To design an interesting tessellation, start with a regular shape that tessellates, such as a triangle or rectangle, and then make little changes, or put your own design inside the shape. Or start with parallel zigzag lines and divide the space between them into identical chunks.

Tessellating toast

Hot toast! WATCH OUT!

Now you can make an interesting tessellated pattern—and then eat it!

BOING!

What to do:

1. Design a tessellating pattern on paper. Don't make it too complicated or it will be hard to cut the toast into shapes.

2. Make several slices of toast. Cover each slice with one of your spreads, making half the slices one color and half the other color.

3. Using a knife or cookie cutter, ask an adult to help you cut the slices of toast into the shapes you need.

4. Arrange your toast tessellation. Take a picture before you eat it!

biscuit cutter

YUM!

If you don't like toast... Make a tessellating pizza instead. Start with a plain tomato sauce and cheese pizza and arrange toppings to make a tessellating pattern.

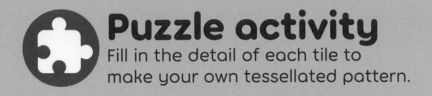

Puzzle activity

Fill in the detail of each tile to
make your own tessellated pattern.

Star gazing

Before you get into bed, take a look up at the night sky. If it's not cloudy—and it is dark—you'll probably see some stars. There are hundreds of billions out there.

How many stars you see from your home depends on where you live. In a city, you might only see 20–30. In the middle of a desert, with no lights around, you might see thousands.

Big numbers are mind-blowing—numbers go on forever. It's not possible to count to the end of numbers since you could always add more. Or you could always double the number you've got to.

600, 000, 000, 000, 000, 000, 000, 000, 000, 000, 000, 000, 000, 000, 000

If you had enough time and patience, you could count all the stars or all the grains of sand on Earth. It would be a very large number: there could be 400 billion stars in our galaxy, the Milky Way. But there are numbers higher.

Scientists work out the number of stars by counting how many are in a small area and multiplying. If they looked at a thousandth of the area of the sky, they would multiply by 1,000 to estimate how many stars there are.

It's difficult to work with very large numbers written out as a long string of digits. Scientific notation shows how many times to multiply by 10, so **1,000,000** is written as **10^6** and **2,000,000** is written as **2×10^6**.

$$1{,}000{,}000 = 10^6$$
$$2{,}000{,}000 = 2 \times 10^6$$

We name numbers that go way beyond what's useful. The number called a googol is 1 followed by 100 zeroes: **10^{100}**. And a googolplex is 1 followed by a googol zeroes, written **10^{googol}**.

$10^{100} =$ 10 000 000 000 000 000
000 000 000 000 000 000 000
000 000 000 000 000 000 000
000 000 000 000 000 000 000
000 000 000 000 000 000 000

Lots and lots and lots

You will need:

- weighing scales
- uncooked rice
- frozen peas
- two small containers or cups
- a calculator
- a pencil and paper

Now you can get an idea of how big numbers of countable things can be—and you don't have to spend too long counting.

What to do:

1. Fill one container with peas and one with rice. How many particles (peas or grains of rice) do you think there are in each container? Write down your guesses.

peas

rice

2. Pour out and weigh the contents of each container. Write down the weights.

weighing scale

3. Now weigh out the smallest amount you can accurately weigh of each substance. This will depend on your scales. Electronic scales can weigh a tiny fraction of an ounce, but otherwise it might be half an ounce.

4. Count the number of peas you have weighed and write down the number. Do the same for the rice grains. If there is too much rice to count, divide the pile roughly in four and count one group of grains, then multiply the answer by 4.

5. Use math to estimate how many particles there are in each of your containers, with help from the calculator. Divide the weight of the contents of the container by the weight of the particles you counted, then multiply by the number of particles you counted. For example:

6. How many particles would there be in 1 lb of each substance? (There are 16 oz in 1 lb. So, if there were 4 oz in the whole container, multiply the total amount of particles you calculated by 4.)

4 oz in whole container ÷ 0.2 oz counted = 20
20 x 50 grains = 1,000

 # Puzzle activity

Match the objects to the numbers in scientific notation that are most likely to go with them. Draw a line to connect the ones that match.

Cats that live in a street

5.4×10^7

Blades of grass in a tennis court

1×10^3

Parking spaces in a multistory car park

10^{16}

Grains of sand on ½ mile of beach

4.3×10^1

You'll find the answers at the back of the book.

Math everywhere!

From morning until night, we see numbers and measurements everywhere. We need math to cook, to travel on time, to build things and to play music. We use math to describe the world around us in quantities.

Imagine a world without math. How would you know how much food costs at the store? How would you know the score of a football game? How would you know when your birthday was if there was no calendar to tell you?

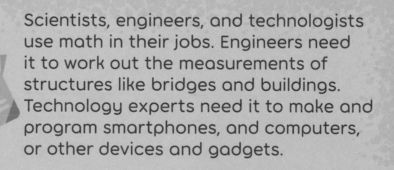

Scientists, engineers, and technologists use math in their jobs. Engineers need it to work out the measurements of structures like bridges and buildings. Technology experts need it to make and program smartphones, and computers, or other devices and gadgets.

Think of all the ways you come across math during your day. Can you think of any maths challenge that you'd like to master? The sky's the limit!

Quiz time!

Test your new maths skills and see how much you've learned with this quick quiz!

1. If your car travels at 40 miles per hour, how far has it gone in 15 minutes?

a) 15 miles ☐
b) 10 miles ☐
c) 55 miles ☐

2. Which of these shapes is symmetrical?

a) b) c)

3. How much change would you get from a $10 bill if you bought a comic for $2.50 and a key ring for $3.50?

a) $7.00 ☐
b) $6.50 ☐
c) $4.00 ☐

4. The length of a sports field is 40 yd and its width is 20 yd. What is its perimeter?

a) 420 yd ☐
b) 800 yd ☐
c) 120 yd ☐

5. If you divided 3 pizzas between 12 people, what fraction of a pizza would each person get?

a) 1/2 ☐
b) 1/4 ☐
c) 1/3 ☐

6. 20 children out of a class of 25 go on a trip to the zoo. What percentage of the class is that?

a) 80% ☐
b) 100% ☐
c) 45% ☐

7. What is -3 + 4?

a) -7 ☐
b) 34 ☐
c) 1 ☐

8. If you make a model of house that is 10 times smaller than its real size, you are using a scale of...

a) 2:10 ☐
b) 1:10 ☐
c) 1:1 ☐

Answers: 1b; 2a; 3c; 4c; 5b; 6a; 7c; 8 b

PUZZLE ACTIVITY ANSWERS

Page 11

1. 4:10
2. 4:35
3. 6:25
4. 6:30
5. 7:20

Page 15

1. Rotated
2. Rotated
3. Reflected
4. Reflected

Page 19

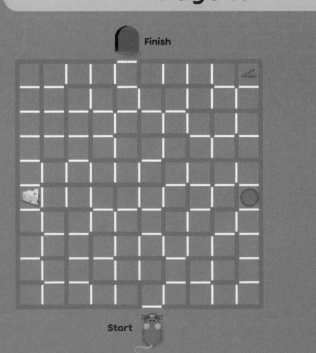

The instructions provided take the mouse to the cheese.

To get it from the cheese to the mouse hole, use these: up 1, right 2, up 3, right 1, down 1, right 1, up 3.

Page 22

1. +20 ft
2. −17 ft
3. −20 ft
4. +30 ft
5. +40 ft
6. +90 ft

Page 27

A. 80 ft
B. 140 ft
C. 156 ft

Page 31

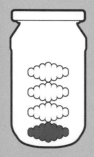 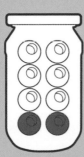   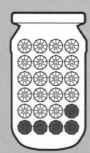

Page 35

Dogs	20%	Birds	20%
Cats	20%	Guinea pigs	25%
Snakes	10%	Tortoises	5%

Page 39

This is just one possible solution. Any other combination of colors will work, as long as there are **4** green beetles. There are **28** beetles in total, so coloring **4** of them green gives you a ½ **chance** of picking a green one. If you add four more beetles and don't color any of them green, you now have a **⅛ chance** of getting a green one.

Page 43

One possible answer is to choose a ball, key ring, zoo animals, sweet and party blower. There are other combinations of items that will also add up to $5.

Page 51

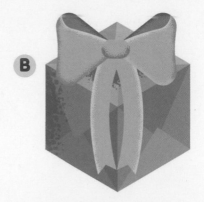

B

5 in x 5 in x 5 in

Page 59

5.4×10^7

1×10^3

10^{16}

4.3×10^1